God
made
easy

BY PATRICE KARST

WARNER ⓦ TREASURES

PUBLISHED BY WARNER BOOKS

A TIME WARNER COMPANY

Warner Books Edition
Copyright © 1996, 1997 by Patrice Karst
All rights reserved.

This Warner Books edition is
published by arrangement with the author.

Warner Treasures® name and logo are
registered trademarks of Warner Books, Inc.
1271 Avenue of the Americas, New York, NY 10020
⨀ A Time Warner Company

Printed in Singapore
First Warner Books Printing: March 1997
10 9 8 7 6 5 4 3 2 1
ISBN: 0-446-91211-5

Acknowledgments

I would like most of all to hug the little girl inside of me who knew so many years ago that there was something really important that God wanted her to say.

Thanks to all those that I love (you know who you are) . . .

—to God, who woke me up and told me to get a pen and start writing. Oh yeah, and who created the universe . . .

—to Amma—Priya loves you . . .

—to Gary Peattie at DeVorss for believing in the book . . .

—to my agents Al Lowman and B. G. Dilworth for being the answer to a prayer . . .

—to my editor Jackie Meyer for jumping in . . .

—to my son and guru, Elijah, whose four-year-old hugs and kisses are the grandest thing that I have ever known . . .

—and to you the reader for opening up your hearts and minds and opening up this book . . .

—to us all!

*Dedicated
to the hope and vision that
all the beings, in all the worlds,
will one day be happy.*

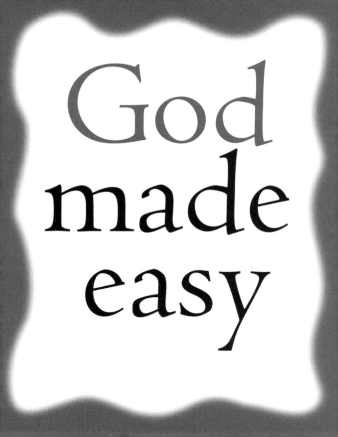

So in case you haven't noticed, the world is feeling pretty crazy lately on every level . . .

Environmental nightmares

Global weird weather and
natural disasters

Crime, Crime, Crime

Hate, Hate, Hate

Economic strife

Drug addictions, alcoholism

Technology growing so fast
you can't keep up

Wars, starvation, AIDS,
killer bees—

We're running on a treadmill
that's going faster and faster.

Changes are happening. It's
time to remember. Has it
gotten your attention yet? . . .

Hey, whoa, stop!

There's good stuff too!

Yep, you're right, it's all here on planet Earth.

Just to name a few:

Rainbows

Shooting stars

Babies

Sex

Hot fudge

The Grand Canyon

Good Comedy

You get the idea . . .

But guess what? There's SOMEONE who's gotten really bad press, a bad rap, all these years—in fact, a lot of us can't even say the name without a bunch of religious dogma pouring through us.

(None of which has anything to do with Him, Her, It, by the way.)

And maybe during all this insanity it's time we all got reacquainted; in fact, maybe that's been part of the problem . . .

. . . Forgetting . . .

Introducing once again . . .
back by popular demand . . .

and need . . .

God

(He* was never really gone, by the way—just forgotten in all the chaos and confusion.)

---

*"He," "She," or "It," whatever you're comfortable with . . . Read on.

Wait! Before you get all charged up and your buttons pushed out of shape . . .

The great news about God is that He has absolutely no ego and will be perfectly content if you wish to call Him instead . . .

Goddess

Supreme Being

Heavenly Father
(or even Big Dad)

Divine Mother

The Creator

Lord

Holy Spirit

Higher Power

The Man Upstairs

A Loving Presence

(there's more)

Almighty

Infinite Intelligence

Universal Energy

Cosmic Consciousness

The Light Within

The Source

Something bigger
than me

You get the idea; just fill in the blank with any name you want.

(Just fill in the blank!)

Trust me,

you'll have a better life.

And here's some more good news:

No religion or spiritual path has an exclusive with God; He is the ultimate independent contractor.

So therefore even if you hear Him called . . .

GAIA (MOTHER EARTH)

ALLAH

KRISHNA

BUDDHA

LAKSHMI

CHRIST

GREAT SPIRIT

SHIVA

KUAN-YIN

RAMA

JEHOVAH

KALI

ADONAI

and the many others . . .

they're all true, and it's all OK.

One God—many different names.

Don't worry, He has absolutely no problem with this, just some fearful, bossy people that feel it's their job to tell you who God is—or isn't.

So how do you get to know
this God, anyway?

Now the fun
begins . . .

Oh, and by the way: the less intellect here, the better. To find God, you've got to get real simple.

What's really
great is God is
everywhere . . .

. . . and there's
nowhere that He
isn't . . .

One place you can start if you're into reading is "the books." Once again, folks, no one book has the only true story, the only right truth.

Some possibilities . . .

The *Bible*

The *Koran*

The *Torah*

The *Bhagavad Gita*

The *Upanishads*

Various spiritual,
metaphysical, New Age titles

One thing, though: books can give you an idea, but to really get *up close and personal* you gotta get your head outta the books and into . . .

Nature

You'll see God and His handi-work all over. Every bird, rock, tree, stream.

Hey, have you ever *really* looked at a flower? Get quiet; you'll hear Him in the silence.

Babies

Just hang out with babies or small children, get real goofy with them and let go.

Voilà! God.

Going Inside

Start a running dialogue with Him. He is, after all, the nearest and the dearest. Just start talking to, crying to, singing to, laughing with, asking why, praying to Him (no formality needed); just take the plunge next time you're feeling sad or scared or lonely. Trust He is listening and tell Him what's up . . .

Then real important: Shut up and

Listen!

Doesn't matter where you are—in bed, at the bus stop, making up your kid's lunchbox, or if you want to get real fancy, make an altar, light a candle, burn incense, put groovy holy pictures up and meditate—the point is, expect to hear Him; then get quiet and give Him a chance to respond.

Churches, Temples, Shrines, Sacred Spots

Lots of good God energy here.

Great Music, Art, Writings

Ain't no way, nohow, a human can do that without some kind of help from above.

Case closed.

Acts of

Kindness, Love,

Support

When we humans are at our best and our hearts are all warm and fuzzy inside . . . you know Who's at work again!

Your Own Conscience

You know that inner stuff that says *Uh-oh! don't do that!* or *Stay away from him* or *Gosh! she looks like she could use a hug!*

Well, guess Who's prompting you?

The Breath

No science allowed, please (it has its place, but in the grand scheme of things unbelievably limited).

Guess what? Twenty-four hours a day SOMETHING is making that heart of yours pump and is breathing your lungs in and out, in and out . . .

Follow It back inside.

Miracles

The phone call that comes at the perfect second.

Being rescued at the last moment.

Those "impossible" coincidences that give you goosebumps (God bumps).

Start watching for them: you'll see even more.

Food

There has got to be Something pretty wonderful in charge of things growing out of dirt that taste that good. Period!

Animals

The colors, varieties, sounds, shapes—all living, breathing, sharing our world. Who do *you* think made 'em?

So why all the
bad stuff?

I know, I know; if there really
is a God, why all the crap? all the
suffering?

Good question . . .

Karma . . .
Balance . . .
Lessons to Learn

Somewhere, sometime, somehow, for every action there was and is a reaction. Also known as "What you sow, you shall reap," or cause and effect. Not always fun, sometimes downright painful, excruciating, yucky . . .

. . . Doesn't mean you can't get mad, pissed off, at God. He doesn't even mind if you scream at Him (remember, no ego).

Perhaps a lot of it remains a mystery till the end; perhaps we can't understand it all right now with our limited human minds . . .

You just have to trust that there is order in the universe and that all will make sense eventually (what else are you gonna do?).

Earth is a school, a place we come to learn what we need to so that we finally get it right, graduate once and for all, and go somewhere else . . .

and now
the best part
of all:

We're going home!!!!

This does not mean that you don't enjoy the ride down here on Earth to its fullest. It just means there's something really *big* to look forward to . . .

Call it what you want . . .

Heaven

Nirvana

Shangri-la

Bliss

Astral plane

"Over there"

Spirit world

The other side

The great beyond

From whence I came

Oh, and by the way—the whole "hell" thing: Unless you've been the worst, most murderous, hideous, evil monster that ever lived, I really wouldn't worry about it . . .

And even if you were, everyone eventually is given a chance to rehabilitate . . .

Worst case: if you weren't great in this life, you might have to come back and do it all over again . . .

. . . maybe.

So now imagine a place with . . .

* No suffering—NONE!

* No cellulite

* No physical illness or injuries

* No death

* No questions unanswered

* No longing not met

* Colors, smells, sights, and sounds that are more beautiful than your wildest imaginings

* Being able to go from here to there anywhere in the cosmos at will

* Seeing and being with all you've ever loved

* Hanging out with GOD on a daily basis . . . effortlessly

* Being happy all the time

* Doing and learning whatever you want

* No cold, no fears, no tears . . .

Wait just a minute!

"Sounds too good to be true; can't be," you say. "Who the hell is this girl and how can she make a promise like this?"

"Anyway, How *dare* she?"

Well, guess what: it's all true, absolutely, every word. I can't prove it to you. That's where that "faith" thing comes in. But quite simply, this has been the message since the beginning of time . . . We're only here on Earth for a short while and then we go home . . . and home is incredible . . .

So if I'm wrong . . . sue me!

(You won't need to.)

Okay,

so what to do while we're still here?

Real simple. Read on . . .

Be kind to all . . .

especially to yourself. The Golden Rule applies here (also known as "Do unto others as you would have them do unto you"). All religions and languages have their version of this rule, by the way. It's a universal thing.

Find and get to know God . . .

Your own heart is the best place to start.

Have fun . . .

There's a lot to do, be, and see here; you might as well make the most out of the visit. And as they say, you only go around once (at least in this body).

Care about what matters . . .

Hint: at the end you won't remember or care much about the money you made, but you *will* about who you loved and who loved you back.

This will become obvious when you start tuning in . . .

Just remember, all you can take with you is *who you became* and *what you learned on your journey*. The rest is maya—illusion.

Be authentic—speak *your* truth . . .

God created you to be uniquely different from anyone else. He had reasons; don't mess with the program.

Try to develop an attitude of gratitude . . .

When you start to see your life in this way, you'll be amazed at how different it can look.

Don't hold grudges . . .

Life really is too short; forgiveness is a good thing (and anyway, it feels better!).

Hang out in the "present" . . .

not the future or the past. Each moment is His gift. (Why do you think it's called "the present"?)

Start to surrender . . .

You may know this as "Thy will be done" or "Let go and let God." The fact is that He who created butterfly wings and the Himalayas knows his stuff—you may want to let Him lead for a change.

Look for the lessons . . .
Learn all you can . . . get wise . . . stay humble.

Lastly, look toward the journey home . . .
Your soul, your being, is here for all eternity . . .

. . . So don't sweat the small stuff.

God bless

Peace be with you

Enjoy the ride

Shalom

Hallelujah

Namaste

Walk in grace and beauty

Om

Peace

Amen

. . . and maybe, just maybe, if we each do our part (and with a little help from Him), this wonderful spinning blue orb on which we all find ourselves can finally heal.

Remember . . .

we're all in this together . . .

. . . more will be revealed . . .

and never, ever forget . . .

you are loved . . .

There is no end . . .